Words for School

Written by Alison Milford

Illustrated by Mike Phillips

Published by Ladybird Books Ltd
A Penguin Company
Penguin Books Ltd, 80 Strand, London WC2R 0RL, UK
Penguin Books Australia Ltd, Camberwell, Victoria, Australia
Penguin Books (NZ) Ltd, Private Bag 102902, NSMC, Auckland, New Zealand

10 9 8 7 6 5 4 3 2 1

ISBN 10: 1-84646-150-2
ISBN 13: 978-1-84646-150-7

©LADYBIRD BOOKS MMVI

Printed in Singapore

Contents

Using this dictionary

This dictionary will help you to:
- Find out what words mean
- Check how words are spelt
- Find out more about the words you are using
- Learn new words about a particular school subject

About this dictionary
- This book is divided into school subjects, making it easy to locate words and understand them in context.
- Every definition is written in simple language so that you will be able to understand the meanings easily.
- Where several definitions might be possible for a word, those most appropriate to the subject area are included to avoid confusion.
- Pictures are used to make definitions even easier to understand.
- At the back of the book lots of extra information is included.
- Some simple grammatical references are included to give you an introduction to the roles played by different types of words.

Finding words
1 Decide what subject area the word you want to look up is in.
2 Using the contents page, go to the start of that subject section.
3 The words are listed in alphabetical order, so look at the first letter of the word you are trying to find, and look through the section until you come to that letter.
4 You can use the guide words at the top of each page to help you find out whether or not you are on the right page.

Using this dictionary for spelling
If you want to remember a spelling from the dictionary you can use this method:
- read the word and remember the spelling
- cover the word
- write the word without looking at it
- uncover the word and check it against the one you have written

Playing the 'dictionary game'
Take turns suggesting a word and letting the other person find it. Who's the quickest?

Key to symbols and grammatical terms

(n) This means that the word is a **noun**. A noun is the word that we use for an object or thing. You can find out more about nouns by looking through the dictionary and seeing which words are nouns.

(v) This means that the word is a **verb**. A verb is a word that describes an action, or when something is done. Look at the verbs in the dictionary to find out more about verbs.

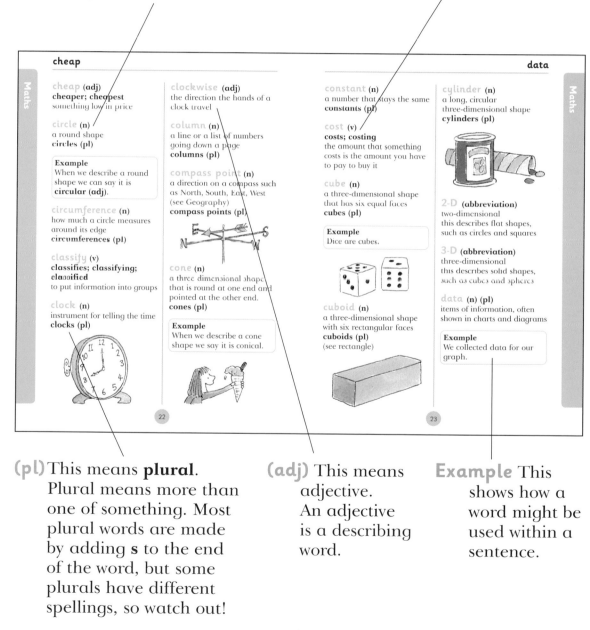

cheap (adj)
cheaper; cheapest
something low in price

circle (n)
a round shape
circles (pl)

Example
When we describe a round shape we can say it is **circular (adj)**.

circumference (n)
how much a circle measures around its edge
circumferences (pl)

classify (v)
classifies; classifying; classified
to put information into groups

clock (n)
instrument for telling the time
clocks (pl)

clockwise (adj)
the direction the hands of a clock travel

column (n)
a line or a list of numbers going down a page
columns (pl)

compass point (n)
a direction on a compass such as North, South, East, West (see Geography)
compass points (pl)

cone (n)
a three dimensional shape that is round at one end and pointed at the other end.
cones (pl)

Example
When we describe a cone shape we say it is conical.

constant (n)
a number that stays the same
constants (pl)

cost (v)
costs; costing
the amount that something costs is the amount you have to pay to buy it

cube (n)
a three-dimensional shape that has six equal faces
cubes (pl)

Example
Dice are cubes.

cuboid (n)
a three-dimensional shape with six rectangular faces
cuboids (pl)
(see rectangle)

cylinder (n)
a long, circular three-dimensional shape
cylinders (pl)

2-D (abbreviation)
two-dimensional
this describes flat shapes, such as circles and squares

3-D (abbreviation)
three-dimensional
this describes solid shapes, such as cubes and spheres

data (n) (pl)
items of information, often shown in charts and diagrams

Example
We collected data for our graph.

22

23

Maths

Maths

(pl) This means **plural**. Plural means more than one of something. Most plural words are made by adding **s** to the end of the word, but some plurals have different spellings, so watch out!

(adj) This means adjective. An adjective is a describing word.

Example This shows how a word might be used within a sentence.

English

account (n)
a description of something that has happened
accounts (pl)

address (n)
the place where someone works or lives
addresses (pl)

Example
You would write an address on an envelope.

adjective (n)
a word that describes what someone or something is like
adjectives (pl)

adverb (n)
a word that tells you how something or someone does things
adverbs (pl)

alliteration (n)
words next or close to each other which start with the same letter or letter sound

alphabet (n)
the set of letters used for writing and reading
alphabets (pl)

alphabetical (adj)
in the order of the letters of the alphabet

Example
School registers and the words in dictionaries are in alphabetical order.

anthology (n)
a collection of poems, writing or music
anthologies (pl)

antonym (n)
a word that means the opposite to another word

> **Example**
> Big is the antonym of small.

author (n)
a person who writes fiction or non-fiction
authors (pl)

blurb (n)
information on the front and back of a book cover telling you what the book or story is about

bold print (n)
letters that are made to look darker to make a word or sentence stand out

capital letter (n)
one of the large letters in the alphabet such as A, B, C, D, used
1. at the beginning of sentences
2. at the beginning of names
3. at the beginning of titles and headings
capital letters (pl)

caption (n)
a comment or description to go with a picture
captions (pl)

chapter (n)
one of the parts into which a book is divided
chapters (pl)

character (n)
1. a person or creature in a story or poem
2. your character is the sort of person you are
characters (pl)

> **Example**
> You can find out what a book character is like by
> • what they say
> • what they do
> • what they look like.

comic strip (n)
a sequence of drawings that tells a story
comic strips (pl)

comma (n)
a punctuation mark (,) used in writing
1. to break up long sentences
2. to put at the end of lines of a poem
3. to come after each item in a list
commas (pl)

compound word (n)
a word made from two other words

> **Example**
> 'Football' and 'handbag' are **compound words (pl)**.

consonant (n)
all the letters of the alphabet except the five vowel letters (see vowel)
consonants (pl)

contents (n)
a list at the front of a book which tells you what is in it
contents (pl)

> **Example**
> The contents for this book is on page 3.

debate (n)
when people talk about their different views on a subject
debates (pl)

definition (n)
a short sentence that explains what a word or phrase means
definitions (pl)

description (n)
1. to explain how something or someone looks
2. to explain what happened
descriptions (pl)

diary (n)
a book in which you write down what you did on each day of the week
diaries (pl)

dictionary (n)
a book that tells you how words are spelt and what they mean

> **Example**
> The words in **dictionaries (pl)** are listed alphabetically.

discussion (n)
to talk with other people about a subject
discussions (pl)

drama (n)
a play performed by actors
dramas (pl)

edit (v)
edits; editing; edited
to change parts of a piece of writing to make it easier or more interesting to read

encyclopedia (n)
a book that has lots of information about one or more topics
encyclopedias (pl)

exclamation mark (n)
a punctuation mark (!) used in writing to show a strong feeling
exclamation marks (pl)

> **Example**
> Watch out! Keep off!

explanatory text (n)
a piece of writing that explains how something works or is an answer to a question
explanatory texts (pl)

> **Example**
> An explanatory text can be about how the Ancient Egyptians built pyramids.

fable (n)
a story that teaches a lesson or moral
fables (pl)

fact (n)
information that is true
facts (pl)

fiction (n)
fiction is made-up stories that are not real
fiction (pl)

first person (n)
something written in your own voice or a character's voice

> **Example**
> I was bored, so I asked my friend over for tea.

flow chart (n)
a diagram which shows the order of something

full stop (n)
a punctuation mark (.) that is put at the end of a sentence
full stops (pl)

genre (n)
a style or type of writing

> **Example**
> There are many types of **genres (pl)** for story writing.

glossary (n)
a list at the back of the book that explains the meanings of words used for different topics
glossaries (pl)

heading (n)
the title at the top of a page
headings (pl)

illustrate (v)
illustrates; illustrating; illustrated
to draw pictures to go with a story or piece of writing

illustration (n)
a picture, usually in a book
illustrations (pl)
Illustrators (n) (pl) draw illustrations.

index (n)
an alphabetical list of subjects found at the back of a book
indexes or **indices** (pl)

information (n)
facts about subjects

information text (n)
writing that tells the reader about things: e.g. how something works, about an event or the findings of a survey
information texts (pl)

instruction (n)
something written or spoken that tells you how to do something
instructions (pl)

Example
Recipes are instructions on how to cook or make food.

joke (n)
a joke is something that you say to make people laugh
jokes (pl)

English

label (n)
a word or sentence on a piece of paper that explains what something is

> **Example**
> Class 2L wrote **labels (pl)** for a display.

layout (n)
the way a story or drawing is set out on a page
layouts (pl)

legend (n)
a story that may have been true but has changed over the years
legends (pl)

letter (n)
1. a sign that we use for writing words, such as a, b, c, d
2. a written or printed message you can send to someone
letters (pl)

list (n)
names, words or numbers written down next to or under each other

> **Example**
> We write **lists (pl)** for shopping, or of our top ten favourite books.

myth (n)
a very old story with gods, goddesses or heroes, used to explain unusual things
myths (pl)

narrative text (n)
recounting an event in a poem or story in the right time order
narrative texts (pl)

non-chronological writing (n)
writing that is not in the correct time order

non-fiction (n)
writing about people and events from real life
non-fiction (pl)

> **Example**
> I like reading non-fiction, such as people's life-stories.

nonsense poem (n)
a silly poem that docs not have a meaning
nonsense poems (pl)

note (n)
a short message or letter
notes (pl)

note (v)
notes; noting; noted
to write down the important parts of something you hear or read

noun (n)
a word that is a name of a place, person or object
nouns (pl)

> **Example**
> 'John', 'London' and 'table' are all nouns.

opinion (n)
the point of view of one or more people
opinions (pl)

paragraph (n)
a section of sentences in a piece of writing
paragraphs (pl)

> **Example**
> We use paragraphs when
> • we change to another idea
> • we change the time or place
> • when a person speaks dialogue.

phrase (n)
two or more words that are used together

> **Example**
> The words 'good evening' and 'see you later' are both **phrases (pl)**.

play (n)
a story for actors to act out on the stage or on the radio
plays (pl)

plot (n)
the main events that happen in a story
plots (pl)

> **Example**
> The main parts of a plot are the:
> • beginning of a story
> • middle of a story
> • ending of a story.

plural (n)
the form of a word that is used to describe more than one thing
plurals (pl)

poem (n)
a piece of writing set out in short lines and verses that may use rhyming words
poems (pl)

poet (n)
someone who writes poems
poets (pl)

prefix (n)
two or three letters put in front of words to change their meanings
prefixes (pl)

project (n)
a piece of work where you find out about something and write about it
projects (pl)

pronoun (n)
a word that is used instead of a noun

> **Example**
> 'He', 'she', 'it', 'me', 'we' and 'they' are all **pronouns (pl)**.

publish (v)
publishes; publishing; published
to print and sell books newspapers or magazines

pun (n)
a fun play on words that sound alike but have different meanings
puns (pl)

> **Example**
> What flowers are on your face? Tulips (two lips).

punctuation (n)
different marks or signs used in writing to help readers understand the meaning of the text

> **Example**
> Full stops and commas are punctuation.

question (n)
what you ask or write when you want to know about something or someone
questions (pl)

report (n)
1. a piece of writing about an event or situation
2. a piece of writing using the information and findings of a project
reports (pl)

review (n)
written or spoken views and ideas about something
reviews (pl)

rhyme (n)
1. a short poem that has words at the end that sound the same
2. words with endings that sound the same
rhymes (pl)

> **Example**
> Can you hear the rhyming words using '–at'?
> The cat sat on the mat.

riddle (n)

a question or statement which forms a puzzle to be solved
riddles (pl)

role play (n)

an acting out of a real life or make-believe event
role plays (pl)

scan (v)
scans; scanning; scanned
1. to read a piece of writing quickly to find the information needed
2. for all the lines of a poem to have the same rhythm

> **Example**
> Aunt Izzy likes the local park,
> We always have such fun.
> We climb and hide and swing and jump,
> And run and run and RUN!

scene (n)
1. different parts of a play
2. the place where something is happening
scenes (pl)

sentence (n)
a group of words that say something

> **Example**
> **Sentences (pl)** begin with a capital letter and end with a full stop.

setting (n)

where a story is set, such as in a castle, a space ship or on the beach
settings (pl)

sign (n)

1. a message made with the body

> **Example**
> He waved his hand as a sign to say 'hello'.

2. a board or notice that gives you information

skim (v)

skims; skimming; skimmed

to quickly read a piece of writing to get the main idea of what it is trying to say

speech bubble (n)

used in pictures when spoken words are in a bubble shape pointing to the speaker
speech bubbles (pl)

speech mark (n)

a punctuation mark (" ") used to show where words are being spoken by characters
speech marks (pl)

> **Example**
> "You need to put speech marks at the beginning and at the end of a piece of dialogue," said Jake.

spelling (n)
the correct order of letters in a word
spellings (pl)

story board (n)
a plan using pictures and writing to show the outline and plot of a story
story boards (pl)

summary (n)
sentences written to give the main points of a piece of writing
summaries (pl)

syllable (n)
one of the sounds or beats in a word

> **Example**
> There are three **syllables (pl)** in bicycle.

synonym (n)
a word that means the same as another word
synonyms (pl)

text (n)
a piece of writing
texts (pl)

theme (n)
a subject or topic that someone writes or speaks about
themes (pl)

third person (n)
to write something in another person's voice or for use in formal letters
(see first person)

> **Example**
> The boy was bored so he asked his friend over for tea.

title (n)
the name of a piece of work such as a book
titles (pl)

> **Example**
> The title of this book is 'Words for School'.

tongue twister (n)
a fun sentence or verse that is hard to say quickly
tongue twisters (pl)

> **Example**
> Try to say this sentence fast. 'She sells seashells on the seashore.'

traditional story (n)
a story that has been passed down through the years
traditional stories (pl)

verb (n)
a word that describes what someone or something is doing
verbs (pl)

jumping

running

throwing

hopping

verse (n)
a group of lines in a poem
verses (pl)

vocabulary (n)
all the words that someone knows and uses
vocabularies (pl)

vowel (n)
the five letters a, e, i, o, u
vowels (pl)

Maths

add (+) (v)
adds; adding; added
to put numbers together

a.m. (adj)
two letters used to show that
a time is in the morning
(also see p.m.)

amount (n)
how much or how many
amounts (pl)

angle (n)
the corner where two lines
meet
angles (pl)

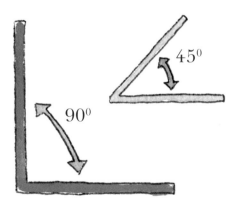

anticlockwise (adj)
travelling in the opposite
direction of a clock's hands

approximate (adj)
an approximate amount is
almost correct but not exact

Example
There were approximately
50 marbles in the jar.
When we guess how
many we make an
approximation (n).

balance (v)
**balances; balancing;
balanced**
to have equal weights on
each side

block graph (n)
a graph that uses solid blocks to show different amounts of things
block graphs (pl)

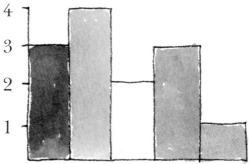

breadth (n)
the distance between two sides of something
breadths (pl)

calculate (v)
calculates; calculating; calculated
to find the answer to a sum

calculation (n)
a sum or answer that has been worked out
calculations (pl)

A **calculator (n)** can help you to make calculations.

capacity (n)
a measure of how much a container can hold
capacities (pl)

centimetre (cm) (n)
a measure
centimetres (pl)

> **Example**
> There are 100 centimetres in a metre.

centre (n)
the middle of something
centres (pl)

chance (n)
something that might happen
chances (pl)

> **Example**
> An equal chance is when something could as easily happen as not.

change (n)
money given back when you pay too much

chart (n)
information in a table
charts (pl)

cheap (adj)
cheaper; cheapest
something low in price

circle (n)
a round shape
circles (pl)

> **Example**
> When we describe a round
> shape we can say it is
> **circular (adj)**.

circumference (n)
how much a circle measures
around its edge
circumferences (pl)

classify (v)
**classifies; classifying;
classified**
to put information into groups

clock (n)
instrument for telling the time
clocks (pl)

clockwise (adj)
the direction the hands of a
clock travel

column (n)
a line or a list of numbers
going down a page
columns (pl)

compass point (n)
a direction on a compass such
as North, South, East, West
(see Geography)
compass points (pl)

cone (n)
a three-dimensional shape
that is round at one end and
pointed at the other end.
cones (pl)

> **Example**
> When we describe a cone
> shape we say it is conical.

constant (n)
a number that stays the same
constants (pl)

cost (v)
costs; costing
the amount that something
costs is the amount you have
to pay to buy it

cube (n)
a three-dimensional shape
that has six equal faces
cubes (pl)

Example
Dice are cubes.

cuboid (n)
a three-dimensional shape
with six rectangular faces
cuboids (pl)
(see rectangle)

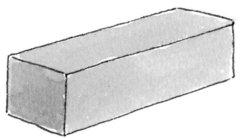

cylinder (n)
a long, circular
three-dimensional shape
cylinders (pl)

2-D (abbreviation)
two-dimensional
this describes flat shapes,
such as circles and squares

3-D (abbreviation)
three-dimensional
this describes solid shapes,
such as cubes and spheres

data (n) (pl)
items of information, often
shown in charts and diagrams

Example
We collected data for our
graph.

day (n)
1. A day is made up of 24 hours
2. the time that it is daylight
days (pl)

decrease (v)
decreases; decreasing; decreased
to become smaller or less

depth (n)
the distance from top to bottom or front to back
depths (pl)

> **Example**
> Rachel measured the depth of the sofa.

diagonal (adj)
a diagonal line goes from one corner of something to the opposite corner
diagonals (pl)

difference (n)
the total left when a smaller number is subtracted from a larger number
differences (pl)

digit (n)
the number symbols of 0, 1, 2, 3, 4, 5, 6, 7, 8, 9
digits (pl)

> **Example**
> 65 is a two-digit number.

digital clock (n)
a clock (often a 24-hour clock) that shows the time in exact numbers, such as 02:45
digital clocks (pl)

distance (n)
the length between two places or points
distances (pl)

divide (÷) (v)
divides, dividing, divided
1. to split something or an amount into parts
2. to find out how many times a number goes into a larger number

Example
Justin divided a cake into 8 pieces. When we divide amounts it is called **division (n)**.

double
doubles; doubling; doubled
1. (v) to multiply a number by 2
(10 doubled is 20)
2. (adj) something that is twice an amount or size

edge (n)
the outside rim of an object or shape
edges (pl)

Example
A square has 4 edges.
A pyramid has 6 or 8 edges.

eighth
1. (adj) when something comes at number eight in a sequence
2. (n) one of eight equal parts
eighths (pl)

equal (=)
the same as
2 + 5 is equal to 7 (2 + 5 = 7)

equal part (n)
a part that is the same size or amount as another part
equal parts (pl)

estimate (v)
estimates; estimating; estimated
to make a close guess

even (adj)
a number that you can divide exactly by 2

> **Example**
> 2, 14, 26, 38 and 40 are all even numbers.

exact (adj)
a number or amount that is just right

> **Example**
> The exact number of marbles in the jar was 425.

exchange (v)
exchanges; exchanging; exchanged
to change a number for another of equal value

> **Example**
> Exchange is also 'carrying' a number when doing sums in addition, subtraction, multiplication and division.

expensive (adj)
costing a lot of money

> **Example**
> A new car is expensive.

face (n)
the flat side or surface of a shape
faces (pl)

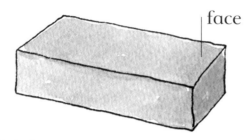

face

fifth
1. **(adj)** when something comes at number five in a sequence
2. **(n)** one of five equal parts
fifths (pl)

figure (n)
a number such as 1, 2, 3, 4
figures (pl)

first (adj)
when something comes before everything else in a sequence

fourth (adj)
when something comes at number four in a sequence

fraction (n)
where a whole number is divided into equal parts

> **Example**
> These numbers are
> **fractions (pl)** – ¼, ⅓, ½.

gram (g) (n)
a measure of weight

> **Example**
> There are 1000 **grams (pl)**
> in 1 kilogram.

graph (n)
a diagram which shows information
graphs (pl)

grid (n)
lines that go horizontally (across) and vertically (down) through each other to make lots of small boxes
grids (pl)

half (½) (n)
one of two equal parts
halves (pl)

> **Example**
> If we cut a pizza straight through the middle we have two halves.

half-hour (n)
thirty minutes
half-hours (pl)

height (n)
how tall something is
heights (pl)

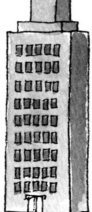

hexagon (n)
a six-sided shape
hexagons (pl)

> **Example**
> Something that is a hexagon shape is
> **hexagonal (adj)**.

horizontal (adj)
something that is horizontal
is flat and level

hour (n)
an hour is made up of sixty
minutes

> **Example**
> The short pointer on a clock
> is the **hour hand (n)**.

hundred (n)
the number 100
hundreds (pl)

increase (v)
**increases; increasing;
increased**
to make something greater

kilogram (kg) (n)
a measure of weight (1000
grams make 1 kilogram)
kilograms (pl)

kilometre (km) (n)
a measure of distance (1000
metres make 1 kilometre)
kilometres (pl)

length (n)
1. the measure from one end
of something to the other
2. the amount of time that
has gone by
lengths (pl)

less (adj)
less is not as much

> **Example**
> How much less is
> 25 than 40? 40 − 25 = 15
> The symbol < means 'less
> than', e.g. 25 < 40

line (n)
a long or short mark
lines (pl)

litre (l) (n)
a measure of liquid (1 litre is
1000 millilitres)
litres (pl)

mass (n)
the weight of an object, in
grams (g) or kilograms (kg)
masses (pl)

measure (v)
measures; measuring; measured
to use standard units to find the size or amount of something

metre (m) (n)
a measure of length (1 metre is 100 centimetres)
metres (pl)

millilitre (ml) (n)
a measure of liquid (There are 1000 **millilitres (pl)** in 1 litre)

minus (−)
another word meaning take away or subtract

minute (n)
a measure of time (there are sixty **minutes (pl)** in one hour)

month (n)
one of the twelve parts that make up one year
A calendar shows the 12 **months (pl)**.

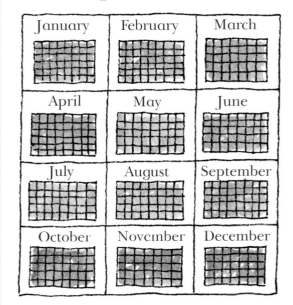

January	February	March
April	May	June
July	August	September
October	November	December

more
a larger amount of something

> **Example**
> Ahmed has 12 apples. How many more would he need to have 24 apples?
> We use the symbol > for the term 'more than'.
> $128 > 110$

multiplication (x) (n)
the act of multiplying numbers
multiplications (pl)

multiply (v)
multiplies; multiplying; multiplied
When you multiply a number you make it a number of times bigger

> **Example**
> 5 times 5 = 25 (5 x 5 = 25)

note (n)
paper money such as £5
notes (pl)

number line (n)
a line with numbers along it arranged in order
number lines (pl)

number square (n)
a grid with numbers in it arranged in order
number squares (pl)

numeral (n)
a symbol meaning a number

> **Example**
> X and V are Roman **numerals (pl)** for 10 and 5

oblong (n)
a rectangular shape
oblongs (pl)

octagon (n)
an eight-sided shape
octagons (pl)

odd (adj)
a number that has one (1) left over when divided by two

> **Example**
> 1, 3, 5, 7, 9 are odd numbers.

order (v)
orders; ordering; ordered
to put numbers in a correct line, pattern or sequence

oval (n)
an egg-shaped object
ovals (pl)

pair (n)
two things that go together
pairs (pl)

pattern (n)
a sequence of numbers or shapes
patterns (pl)

pentagon (n)
a five-sided shape
pentagons (pl)

Something that is a pentagon shape is **pentagonal (adj)**.

plus (+)
the symbol used for addition such as 234 + 45

polygon (n)
a shape with three or more straight sides and angles
polygons (pl)

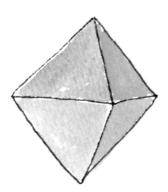

p.m. (adj)
two letters used to show that a time is in the afternoon

price (n)
the cost of something
prices (pl)

> **Example**
> The price of Zoë's coat was £12 and the price of Mila's coat was £14.

prism (n)
a prism is made up of regular polygons (see polygons)
prisms (pl)

probable (adj)
something likely to happen
Something unlikely to happen is **improbable (adj)**.

product (n)
the total when you multiply different amounts together
products (pl)

pyramid (n)
a 3-D solid shape with three or four sides and a base
pyramids (pl)

quarter (¼) (n)
one of four equal parts
quarters (pl)

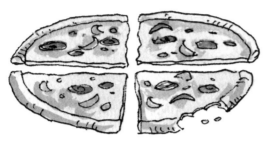

rectangle (n)
a four-sided shape with four right angles
rectangles (pl)

reflection (n)
an image shown in a mirror
reflections (pl)

regular shape (n)
with equal sides and angles
regular shapes (pl)

remainder (n)
the number left over once a number has been divided into another one
remainders (pl)

right angle (n)
an angle that measures 90 degrees
right angles (pl)

rotate (v)
rotates; rotating; rotated
to move a shape or line around a point or axis

round (v)
rounds; rounding; rounded
to go up or down to the nearest number, e.g. round 19 up to 20

scales (n)
a machine to weigh things
scales (pl)

season (n)
the four parts of the year, which are spring, summer, autumn and winter
seasons (pl)

second
1. **(adj)** number two in a sequence
2. **(n)** a measure of time
seconds (pl)

semicircle (n)
half a circle
semicircles (pl)

sequence (n)
an order that numbers or amounts are put in
sequences (pl)

set (n)
a group of things, often alike
sets (pl)

share (v)
shares; sharing; shared
to divide something up between two or more people

> **Example**
> If four apples are shared equally between two children, then each child will get two apples.

short (adj)
something short is not long

> **Example**
> A ribbon measuring 20 cm is shorter (less long) than a ribbon measuring 30 cm.

sideways
a movement from one side to another

sign (n)
a symbol or character which gives mathematical information
signs (pl)

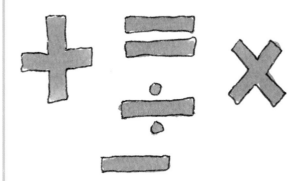

similar (adj)
very much alike

single (adj)
one on its own

size (n)
how big or small something is
sizes (pl)

slide (v)
slides; sliding; slid
to move smoothly over a surface

sort (v)
sorts; sorting; sorted
to group things according to a set of rules, such as colour, shape, size, weight and so on

Maths

sphere (n)
a solid round ball
spheres (pl)

square (n)
a shape with four equal sides
and four right angles
squares (pl)

standard unit (n)
an exact unit of
measurement used by most
people, e.g. a centimetre

Example
Inches and centimetres are
different kinds of
standard units (pl).

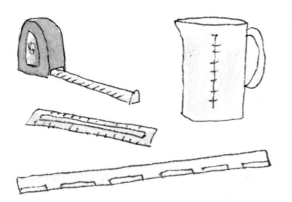

subtract (-) (v)
**subtracts; subtracting;
subtracted**
to take away one number
from another number

Example
When you subtract
25 from 100 you get 75.
$(100 - 25 = 75)$

subtraction (n)
when we take away numbers
subtractions (pl)

sum (n)
1. an amount of money
2. the total of numbers
added together
sums (pl)

symmetrical (adj)
if something is symmetrical
you can divide it into two
equal and matching halves

take away (v)
a way of saying 'subtract'

Example
Sixty-four take away
thirty-four equals thirty.
$(64 - 34 = 30)$

ten (n)
the number 10

> **Example**
> There are 10 **tens (pl)** in a
> hundred.

ten thousand (n)
the number 10,000
100 x 100 makes ten thousand.

tenth
1. **(adj)** when something
comes at number ten in a
sequence
2. **(n)** one of ten equal parts
tenths (pl)

third
1. **(adj)** when something
comes at number three in a
sequence
2. **(n)** one of three equal parts

> **Example**
> We can show **thirds (pl)** in
> fractions ⅓, ⅔.

thousand (n)
the number 1000
10 x 100 makes 1000.
thousands (pl)

time (n)
a measure of hours, minutes,
seconds and days, months
and years
times (pl)

> **Example**
> The time the train was due
> was 8.30 p.m. but it
> arrived at 9.00 p.m.

times (n)
1. how many times one
number goes into another
2. how much something is
bigger or shorter

> **Example**
> The branch was three times
> the length of my arm.

Maths

times-table (n)
sequences of figures that help you work out sums quickly and correctly
times-tables (pl)

total (n)
the final amount or number
totals (pl)

triangle (n)
a flat shape with three straight sides and three angles
triangles (pl)

turn (v)
turns; turning; turned
to move around a point or axis

unit (n)
The units of a number are the ones
units (pl)

vertical (adj)
a line from top to bottom

weigh (v)
weighs; weighing; weighed
to find out how heavy or light something is

width (n)
the distance from side to side of an object
widths (pl)

> **Example**
> The width of the first bed is too narrow and the width of the other bed is too wide.

year (n)
the period of 365 days (366 for leap year) from January to December
years (pl)

Science

absorbent (**adj**)
something which soaks up liquids easily

adapt (**v**)
adapts; adapting; adapted; adaptation (**n**)
to fit in with the surroundings (see camouflage) to make it hard to be seen

> **Example**
> Desert plants have adapted to the lack of water.

air (**n**)
the mix of invisible gases which we breathe

amphibian (**n**)
a creature that can live in water and on land
amphibians (**pl**)

antenna (**n**)
two long thin pointers on the top of an insect's head to help it feel the area around it
antennae (**pl**)

antennae
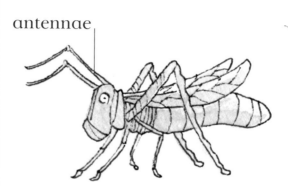

apparatus (**n**)
tools and materials needed for a science experiment
apparatus (**pl**)

> **Example**
> The apparatus needed to study mini-beasts was a magnifier and a jam jar.

asteroid (**n**)
a small planet
asteroids (**pl**)

battery (n)
an object that stores electricity
batteries (pl)

beam (n)
a line or ray of light
beams (pl)

boil (v)
boils; boiling; boiled
to reach the temperature where liquid turns into a vapour

> **Example**
> When water becomes very hot, it starts to boil and bubble.

bone (n)
the hard white part inside the body of some animals which makes up a skeleton
bones (pl)

brain (n)
the part of a body which controls your body and which allows it to think
brains (pl)

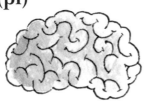

breathe (v)
breathes; breathing; breathed
to take air into the body and then let it out

bright (adj)
something that gives out or reflects light

bubble (n)
a ball of liquid filled with air or gas
bubbles (pl)

bulb (n)
the onion-like base of some plants, found under the ground
bulbs (pl)

buzzer (n)
an object that makes a sound when electricity flows into it
buzzers (pl)

camouflage (v)
camouflages; camouflaging; camouflaged
the way some animals use their shape or colour to blend into the background

canine (n)
1. a kind of sharp tooth
2. the dog family
canines (pl)

carbohydrate (n)
something in a group of foods that gives a body energy

> **Example**
> Bread, potato and pasta contain lots of
> **carbohydrates (pl)**.

carnivore (n)
an animal that eats only meat
carnivores (pl)

caterpillar (n)
a worm-shaped creature that turns into a butterfly or a moth (see life cycle)
caterpillars (pl)

chrysalis (n)
(also known as a pupa) the hard shell a caterpillar makes for itself before it turns into a butterfly or moth (see life cycle)
chrysalises (pl)

circuit (n)
a path for electricity to flow around
circuits (pl)

comet (n)
an object that moves around the solar system or space
comets (pl)

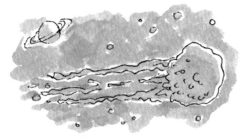

compost (n) (pl)
a mix of decaying plant materials used for making the soil good for growing plants

conduct (v)
conducts; conducting; conducted
to carry or transmit heat or electricity

conductor (n)
a material or object that carries or transmits electricity or heat

Example
Lightning **conductors (pl)** are strips of metal that safely carry the electricity from lightning into the ground.

cool
1. **(v) cools; cooling; cooled**
to get colder
2. **(adj)** slightly cold

dark (adj)
with little or no light

decay (v)
decays; decaying; decayed
when something rots or wastes away

Example
If we eat too many sweets, our teeth can decay.

dental (adj)
to do with teeth

dentist (n)
a person who looks after people's teeth
dentists (pl)

diet
1. **(n)** the kind of foods that a person or animal eats
diets (pl)
2. **(v) diets; dieting; dieted**
to avoid certain types of foods in order to lose weight or to be healthier

dinosaur (n)

a kind of reptile that lived millions of years ago (see reptile)

dinosaurs (pl)

dissolve (v)

dissolves; dissolving; dissolved

when a solid mixes and disappears into a liquid

> **Example**
> Sugar dissolves in water but sand doesn't.

egg (n)

an oval or round object laid by birds, reptiles, fish and insects, inside which the young form

eggs (pl)

electricity (n)

a kind of power

enamel (n)

a hard, white coating which protects teeth (see tooth)

enamels (pl)

energy (n)

1. the fitness and strength to do different things

energies (pl)

2. power from things such as heat and electricity, which makes things work

evaporate (v)

evaporates; evaporating; evaporated

for a liquid to change into a vapour

> **Example**
> Hot water evaporates and becomes water vapour.

exercise (v)

exercises; exercising; exercised

to move your body to keep it fit and healthy

experiment (n)
a way to test out an idea or fact and see what happens
experiments (pl)

fish (n)
an animal that swims in the water and uses gills to breathe in water, rather than lungs to breathe in air
fish (pl)

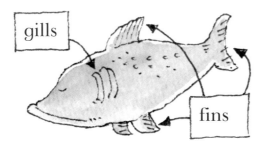

gills

fins

flexible (adj)
easy to bend, e.g. thin plastic or a piece of wire

float (v)
floats; floating; floated
to stay on the surface of a liquid, and not sink

Example
Boats and feathers float on water.

flower (n)
the colourful part of a plant which carries the seeds (see plant)
flowers (pl)

force (n)
the power that pushes or pulls an object
forces (pl)

freeze (v)
freezes; freezing; frozen
to turn a liquid such as water into a solid by making it very cold

Example
We can freeze water in the freezer to make ice cubes.

friction (n)
the force that occurs when one surface rubs against another and stops it sliding

frogspawn (n) (pl)
a lump of frog's eggs covered in a clear jelly

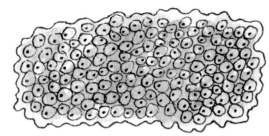

fruit (n)
the seed-carrying part of a flowering plant
fruits (pl)

gas (n)
something that is not a liquid or a solid and is usually clear like air
gases (pl)

germ (n)
a very small living thing that can make you ill if it gets inside your body

> **Example**
> We can catch colds and coughs from **germs (pl)**.

germinate (v)
germinates; germinating; germinated
for a seed to begin to grow

grow (v)
grows; growing; grew
to get bigger
The way things grow is called **growth (n)**.

habitat (n)
the normal area where a plant or animal lives and grows

> **Example**
> The usual **habitats (pl)** for squirrels are places with trees.

hatch (v)
hatches; hatching; hatched
to come out of an egg

healthy (adj)
to be fit and well
If we don't look after ourselves we could become **unhealthy (adj)**.

heart (n)
the part of the body where blood is pumped around
hearts (pl)

heat (n)
the feeling of something being hot or warm
heat (pl)

heat (v)
heats; heating; heated
making something warm or hot

herbivore (n)
an animal that eats only grass or other kinds of plants

> **Example**
> Cows and sheep are **herbivores (pl)**.

hibernate (v)
hibernates; hibernating; hibernated
to spend the winter in a deep type of sleep

> **Example**
> Bears, tortoises and hedgehogs all hibernate.

human
1. **(n)** a man, woman or child
humans (pl)
2. **(adj)** everything that is to do with being a human

ice (n)
frozen water

incisor (n)
a tooth at the front of the mouth, used for cutting food (see tooth)
incisors (pl)

insect (n)
a small creature with six legs, one or two pairs of wings and two antennae

> **Example**
> Ladybirds, flies and butterflies are all **insects (pl)**.

invertebrate (n)
an animal with no backbone, such as a worm
invertebrates (pl)

investigate (v)
investigates; investigating; investigated
to find out the answer to a question or find out information about something

leaf (n)
the green parts of a plant found on the stem (see plant)
leaves (pl)

life cycle (n)
the changes an animal or a plant goes through from the time it forms to when it dies
life cycles (pl)

butterfly life cycle

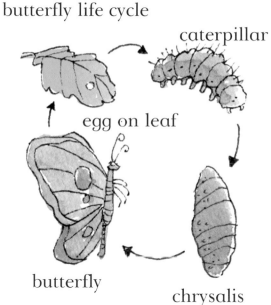

caterpillar

egg on leaf

butterfly

chrysalis

light
1. **(n)** a form of energy that comes from the sun, the stars, fires and lamps making it possible to see
2. **(adj)** not dark, not heavy

liquid (n)
something that is like water
liquids (pl)

lung (n)
the organ inside the chest we use when we breathe
lungs (pl)

magnet (n)
a piece of a certain metal (usually iron) that can pull other metal things towards it
magnets (pl)

magnifier (n)
see-through plastic or glass lens which makes things look bigger

> **Example**
> We can also use a **magnifying (adj)** glass.

magnify (v)
magnifies; magnifying; magnified
to make bigger

mammal (n)
an animal with fur or hair that gives birth and feeds its babies with its own milk

> **Example**
> Cows, people and dogs are all **mammals (pl)**.

material (n)
what something is made of or from (see natural material)
We can change the shape of some **materials (pl)**.

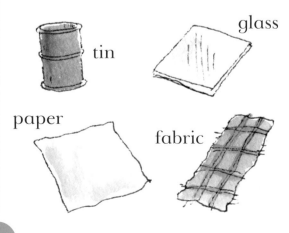

tin

glass

paper

fabric

meat (n)
the flesh from animals that can be eaten
meats (pl)

medicine (n)
something you take when you are ill to make you better
medicines (pl)

melt (v)
melts; melting; melted
when a solid becomes liquid from heating

> **Example**
> Chocolate melts when it is heated.

metal (n)
a hard, solid material
Iron, gold and silver are all
metals (pl).

iron   gold

silver

meteor (n)
a large piece of rock that flies through space
meteors (pl)

microscope (n)
an instrument to look closely at small objects
microscopes (pl)

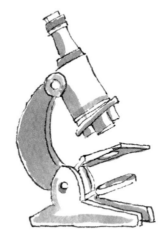

migrate (v)
migrates; migrating; migrated
when birds or other animals travel to another area at a certain time of year

moon (n)
a large bright object we can see in the night sky
moons (pl)

muscle (n)
a thin, strong thread-like material inside the body which allows the body to move easily
muscles (pl)

natural material (n)
a material that comes from nature and is not made by humans
natural materials (pl)

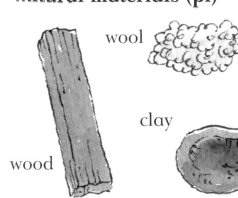

wool

clay

wood

observe (v)
observes; observing; observed
to watch something and take notes

omnivore (n)
an animal that eats both meat and plants
omnivores (pl)

opaque (adj)
not see-through

orbit (n)
when something is moving around a planet
orbits (pl)

planet (n)
a large object in space that moves around a star
planets (pl)

> **Example**
> Planet Earth moves around a star called the Sun.

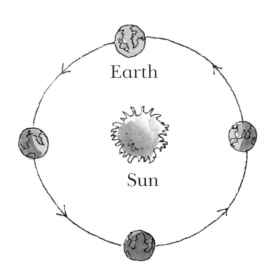

Earth

Sun

plant (n)
a plant is anything that lives that is not an animal

> **Example**
> **Plants (pl)** need sunshine and water to grow.

predict (v)
predicts; predicting; predicted
to guess what is going to happen

pull (v)
pulls; pulling; pulled
to move something towards
you: the opposite of push

push (v)
pushes; pushing; pushed
to move something away
from you: the opposite of pull

record (v)
records; recording; recorded
to write down results of an
experiment or a test

reflect (v)
reflects; reflecting; reflected
to bend or throw back heat,
sound or light rays

> **Example**
> An echo happens when a
> sound reaches a hard
> surface and is reflected
> back, so it can be heard
> again.

reflection (n)
what you see when you look
into the mirror
reflections (pl)

reproduce (v)
**reproduces; reproducing;
reproduced**
to make new life

reptile (n)
a cold-blooded animal with
a backbone

> **Example**
> Snakes, crocodiles and
> tortoises are all
> **reptiles (pl)**.

result (n)
the findings of a test,
observation or experiment
results (pl)

root (n)
1. the underground part of a
plant that draws up water
2. the part of a tooth that
holds it in the gum (see tooth)
roots (pl)

sand (n)
tiny grains of worn-down
stones, usually found
on beaches and in the desert
sand (pl)

seed (n)
the part of a plant that can
grow into a new plant (see
plant)
seeds (pl)

sense (n)
something we use to see, feel,
hear, taste or smell
senses (pl)

shadow (n)
a dark shape which is made
when light falls on something
shadows (pl)

shell (n)
the hard covering of some
animals, eggs or nuts
shells (pl)

shoot (n)
a new part of a plant that
sticks out of the earth or soil
shoots (pl)

sink (v)
sinks; sinking; sunk
to go under the water
(the opposite of float)

skeleton (n)
all the bones that give a body
its shape
skeletons (pl)

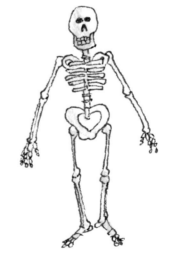

skin (n)
the outer covering of a body
which protects its insides

Example
People used to dress in the
skins (pl) of animals, such
as wolves and bears.

socket (n)
the fixture into which an electric plug is pushed
sockets (pl)

soil (n)
the top covering of the ground
soils (pl)

solar system (n)
the Sun and all the planets that orbit it, and everything that orbits the planets
solar systems (pl)

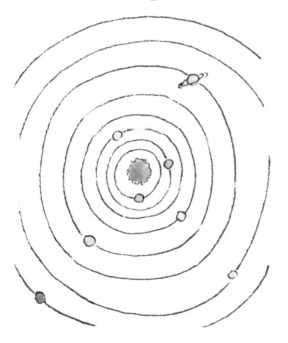

solid (n)
something hard and firm that is not a liquid or a gas
solids (pl)

specimen (n)
an example of something you are studying

> **Example**
> Alex looked at his different **specimens** (pl) of soil.

spider (n)
an eight-legged creature which usually makes webs
spiders (pl)

spring (n)
a piece of metal or plastic which snaps back into position after being pulled up or down
springs (pl)

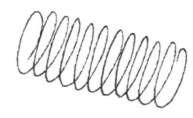

star (n)
a very distant sun that shines in the night sky
stars (pl)

starch (n)
a substance found in foods such as cereals
starches (pl)

steam (n)
the vapour that comes from hot water

sugar (n)
a sweet substance that can give you energy
sugars (pl)

sun (n)
a round object in space that gives us light and heat – it is our nearest star
suns (pl)

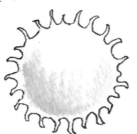

surface (n)
1. the outer part of something
2. the top part of something
surfaces (pl)

Example
Boats sail on the surface of the water.

switch (n)
an object that makes or breaks the flow of electricity through a circuit (see circuit)
switches (pl)

temperature (n)
how cold or hot something is
temperatures (pl)

test (v)
tests; testing; tested
to see how something works or behaves

Example
In science, you need to make sure you do a fair test to get the right result.

thermometer (n)
an instrument that measures how hot or cold something is by showing its temperature
thermometers (pl)

tooth (n)
a hard, white, bone-like point in a mouth, used for biting and chewing
teeth (pl)

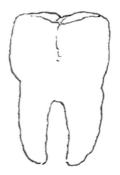

transparent (adj)
when something is see-through, like clear glass

tree (n)
a tall plant with a trunk made of wood and branches, twigs and leaves

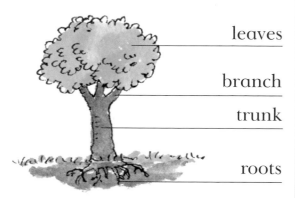

leaves

branch

trunk

roots

variation (n)
a change in something such as a colour, size or shape
variations (pl)

vegetable (n)
a plant that we can eat
vegetables (pl)

vegetarian (n)
someone who eats no meat or fish
vegetarians (pl)

vertebrate (n)
animal with a backbone (or spine)

Example
Humans, lions, fish and birds are all **vertebrates (pl)**.

vitamin (n)
something in food and drink to help a body stay healthy
vitamins (pl)

Example
Vitamin C is good for the skin and helping a body fight disease.

History

AD (Anno Domini)
the years after Jesus Christ was born

> **Example**
> Queen Elizabeth I died in AD 1603.

air raid (n)
a bomb or gas attack by enemy aircraft
air raids (pl)

Allies (the) (n) (pl)
the nations, including Britain, the USA and the Soviet Union, that united against Germany, Italy and Japan in World War II

ancestor (n)
a member of your family who lived long ago
ancestors (pl)

ancient (adj)
1. something which is extremely old
2. belonging to a time long ago, such as Ancient Greece

Anderson shelter (n)
a World War II air raid shelter that was built in people's gardens
Anderson shelters (pl)

Anglo-Saxon

1. **(n)** someone from the Germanic countries who settled in England from around the AD 400s to 1066

> **Example**
> The **Anglo-Saxons (pl)** came to Britain in AD 450 and were its main rulers until AD 1066.

2. **(adj)** something that comes from the Anglo-Saxon times

archaeologist (n)

someone who studies objects or places from the past by digging in chosen areas
archaeologists (pl)

artefact (n)

something from the past that was made by humans
artefacts (pl)

basilica (n)

1. a Roman long palace
2. a Roman long hall used for trade and judging court cases
3. a large church

> **Example**
> Ancient Rome had many **basilicas (pl)**.

battle (n)

a fight between two large groups or armies
battles (pl)

Battle of Britain (n)

a famous World War II air battle, fought from July to September in 1940, between the British Royal Air Force (RAF) and the German Air Force (the Luftwaffe)

BC (Before Christ)

the years before Jesus Christ was born

> **Example**
> The Egyptian pharaoh, Tutankhamun, died in 1327 BC.

belief (n)

people's religious thoughts and ideas
beliefs (pl)

blackout (n)

a World War II rule that everyone had to cover up their lights at night so that enemy planes could not see them
blackouts (pl)

Blitz (n)

the German name for 'lightning war', given to the bombing of British towns and cities between September 1940 and May 1941

burial mound (n)

a small man-made hill where someone is buried
burial mounds (pl)

> **Example**
> Many riches and artefacts were found in the Saxon burial mound at Sutton Hoo.

Catholic

1. **(n)** someone who follows the beliefs and ideas of the Roman Catholic Church
2. **(adj)** the set of religious beliefs followed by Catholics

Celt (n)

a member of a group of people who settled in Britain before the Romans
Celts (pl)

Celtic (adj)

things that are to do with the Celts, such as Celtic crafts

centurion (n)

a Roman army officer who was in charge of a century (see century)
centurions (pl)

century (n)

1. a group of 100 Roman soldiers
2. one hundred years
centuries (pl)

chieftain (n)

a head of a clan or tribe of people, such as the Celts
chieftains (pl)

Christian (n)

someone who believes in the teachings of Jesus Christ and the Bible

Christianity (n) is the religion that **Christians (pl)** follow.

chronology (n)

a list of events and people in the past, set out in the right time order
chronologies (pl)

church (n)

a place where Christians worship
churches (pl)

concentration camp (n)

a prison camp, often used during a war, where people who are not soldiers are kept and treated cruelly

> **Example**
> Many people died in the Nazi **concentration camps (pl)** during World War II.

conquer (v)
conquers; conquering; conquered
to take over other nations and places by force

conquest (n)
to have taken over a place or a nation by force
conquests (pl)

> **Example**
> The Norman Conquest of England was in AD 1066.

court (n)
1. the group of nobles and ladies who served a king or queen

2. a place where trials are held to judge those people who may have broken the law
courts (pl)

courtier (n)
a noble man or lady who is part of a king's or queen's court
courtiers (pl)

Danelaw (n)
the area of England where the Vikings lived between the 800s and the 1000s AD

Danelaw

Danes (n) (pl)
people from Denmark (see Norse and Viking)

D-Day (n)
the 1944 invasion of Europe by Britain and its allies in World War II

decade (n)
a period of 10 years such as the 1940s
decades (pl)

dissolution (n)
the breaking up and destruction of the monasteries in England by Henry VIII

document (n)
a piece of writing that can give information or evidence about something
documents (pl)

> **Example**
> A document can be useful to a historian who wants to find out about something.

doodlebug (n)
a World War II German flying bomb, which did not need a pilot
doodlebugs (pl)

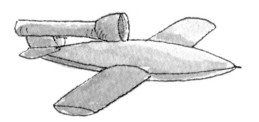

embalm (v)
embalms; embalming; embalmed
to stop a dead body from rotting by treating it with lotions and chemicals

emigrate (v)
emigrates; emigrating; emigrated
to leave one's own country to live somewhere else
Emigration (n) is when someone leaves their own country.
People who emigrate are called **emigrants (pl)**.

emperor (n)
the head of an empire
A woman who rules an empire is called an **empress (n)**.
emperors and **empresses (pl)**

> **Example**
> Julius Caesar was a Roman emperor.

empire (n)
many countries ruled by one country or ruler
empires (pl)

History

evacuate (v)
evacuates; evacuating; evacuated
to move away from a place of danger

> **Example**
> During World War II, many children were evacuated from the cities to the countryside to escape the bomb attacks.

evidence (n) (pl)
information that shows that something could be true, or how it happened

excavation (n)
a place where archaeologists dig and study objects and buildings from the past
excavations (pl)

execution (n)
the act of putting someone to death after they have been found guilty by a law court
executions (pl)

eyewitness (n)
someone who sees an event and writes about it or tells others what they have seen
eyewitnesses (pl)

family tree
a simple chart that gives information about someone's parents, grandparents and other ancestors
family trees (pl)

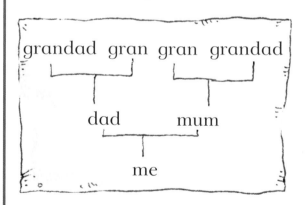

forum (n)
a Roman market place where people met and talked
forums (pl)

History

gas mask (n)
a mask put over the face to help people breathe during poison gas attacks
gas masks (pl)

gladiator (n)
someone from Roman times who would fight for other people's entertainment
gladiators (pl)

god (n)
a male person or thing that people worship
A female god is called a **goddess (n)**.
gods (pl) and **goddesses (pl)**

government (n)
the group of people who run a country
governments (pl)

grandparent (n)
the mother or father of one of your parents
grandparents (pl)

great-grandparent (n)
the mother or father of one of your grandparents
great-grandparents (pl)

heir (n)
someone who inherits or will inherit something, e.g. money

> **Example**
> The man's two children were his **heirs (pl)**.

hieroglyph (n)
a picture or symbol used in Ancient Egyptian writing
hieroglyphs (pl)

historian (n)
someone who studies and finds out about the past
historians (pl)

illuminated writing (n)
hand-written pages
decorated with colourful
designs
illuminated writings (pl)

immigrant (n)
someone who settles in
another country
immigrants (pl)

immigrate (v)
**immigrates; immigrating;
immigrated**
to settle into another country

immigration (n)
settlement in another country

inscription (n)
words, signs or marks, usually
found on stone, wood, metal,
clay and paper

> **Example**
> Many **inscriptions (pl)**
> can be seen on tombs
> from Ancient Egypt.

invade (v)
invades; invading; invaded
to go into a country as an
enemy and take it over

inventory (n)
a list of goods in a house
inventories (pl)

king (n)
a man who rules a land,
often because his father
or mother ruled, and who
often wears a crown as a
sign of power
kings (pl)

Henry VIII

kingdom (n)
a land ruled by a king
or queen
kingdoms (pl)

Latin (n)
the Roman language

law (n)
a rule everyone has to obey
laws (pl)

legion (n)
a group of 3000 to 6000
Roman soldiers

The name we give to soldiers
in Roman **legions (pl)** is
legionnaires (pl).

longship (n)
a Viking ship (see Vikings),
used to travel across the sea
longships (pl)

manuscript (n)
a book written by hand

> **Example**
> The monks in the
> monastery wrote
> **manuscripts (pl)**.

modern (adj)
up-to-date and in the present

monarch (n)
the head of the country or
state such as a king or queen
monarchs (pl)

monastery (n)
a place where monks live,
work and pray
monasteries (pl)

monk (n)
a man who lives a religious
life in a monastery
monks (pl)

mummy (n)
a dead body that has been
embalmed (see embalmed)
and dried to stop it from
rotting

> **Example**
> The Ancient Egyptians
> made **mummies (pl)**.

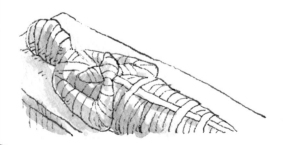

Norse

1. **(adj)** people from Norway, Sweden or Denmark
2. **(n)** the old language spoken by the people of Norway, Sweden and Denmark (see Danes and Viking)

pagan (n)

someone who follows a religion that is not one of the world's main religions

> **Example**
> The Anglo-Saxons were seen as **pagans (pl)** because they believed in many gods.

papyrus (n)

a type of paper used by the Ancient Egyptians, made from a type of grass
papyri or **papyruses (pl)**

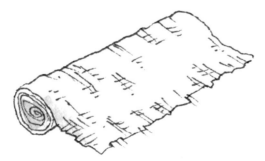

parliament (n)

a group of people chosen to make laws for a country
parliaments (pl)

peasant (n)

a poor labourer who lived mainly in the countryside
peasants (pl)

pharaoh (n)

a ruler in Ancient Egypt
pharaohs (pl)

plague (n)

an outbreak of disease, often spread by rat fleas, which killed many people
plagues (pl)

pope (n)
the chosen head of the Roman Catholic Church (see Catholic)
popes (pl)

primary source (n)
written information, pictures and artefacts made by people at the time and used by historians
primary sources (pl)

> **Example**
> Diaries, letters, inventories and inscriptions are all types of primary sources.

Protestant
1. **(adj)** a kind of Christian church that does not follow the Roman Catholic Church
2. **(n)** someone who follows Protestant church beliefs and ideas
Protestants (pl)

province (n)
a part of an empire or country that has its own government
provinces (pl)

pyramid (n)
a large, pointed building with a square or triangle-shaped base, usually made for a king or queen's tomb
pyramids (pl)

queen (n)
a woman who rules a country or kingdom

> **Example**
> Queen Elizabeth I and Queen Victoria were English **queens (pl)**.

ration (n)
a share of something, such as food, for each person when there isn't much to go around

> **Example**
> During World War II, British people had to have food **rations (pl)**.

refugee (n)
someone who has had to leave their country because of war or some other danger, or because of natural disasters such as flooding
refugees (pl)

reign (n)
the time during which a king or queen rules
reigns (pl)

religion (n)
the ideas and beliefs of people about a god or gods
religions (pl)

research (n)
the act of finding out about something
research (pl)

revolt (n)
to go against the main rulers of a country or region
revolts (pl)

Roman (adj)
a word used to describe the people and things from Ancient Roman times, such as a Roman road

ruin (n)
an old building or place which has fallen down
ruins (pl)

saga (n)
a long, spoken story about heroes and battles, told by Norse people (see Danes, Norse and Viking)

> **Example**
> The Viking warriors listened to **sagas (pl)** before they went to battle.

secondary source (n)
books and other information written about a period or event after it has happened

> **Example**
> Non-fiction books, reports, CD-ROMs and pictures are all types of **secondary sources (pl)**.

settlement (n)
a small village or town where people have decided to settle
settlements (pl)

slave (n)
someone who is owned by another person

> **Example**
> The Egyptians owned many **slaves (pl)**, who built the Great Pyramids of Giza.

sphinx (n)
an Ancient Egyptian statue that has a lion's body and a person's or animal's head
sphinxes (pl)

temple (n)
a place of worship
temples (pl)

time line (n)
a line of dates arranged in order, showing the main events in a period of history
time lines (pl)

tomb (n)
a built place where a dead person is buried
tombs (pl)

tradition (n)
something done for many years in a certain way

> **Example**
> The ways people celebrate Christmas and Diwali are examples of **traditions (pl)**.

tribe (n)
a close group or family of people who are usually ruled by a chief
tribes (pl)

truce (n)
an agreement between enemies to stop fighting at the same time
truces (pl)

Tudor (adj)
the name of the period of history in England from AD 1485 to 1603

Victorian (adj)
anything made at the time of the reign of Queen Victoria

Example
The Victorian period in Britain started in 1837 and ended in 1901.

Viking (n)
raiders, traders and seagoers from Norway, Sweden and Denmark long ago
Vikings (pl)

villa (n)
a large Roman country house

Example
Archaeologists have found the remains of Roman **villas (pl)**.

warrior (n)
a soldier or fighter
warriors (pl)

World War II (n)
a war fought from 1939 to 1945, between the Allies and Germany, Italy and Japan

Geography

agriculture (n)
the production of crops and breeding of livestock
agriculture (pl)

aqueduct (n)
a bridge that carries water
aqueducts (pl)

Arctic
1. **(n)** the area around the North Pole
2. **(adj)** a word that describes weather that is extremely cold

area (n)
1. a piece of land or ground
2. a place or region

Example
All the schools studied their local **areas (pl)** when they worked on their local history projects.

atlas (n)
a book of maps
atlases (pl)

bay (n)
a wide piece of land by the sea or ocean which curves inwards
bays (pl)

beach (n)
the shore of a sea, lake or ocean which is covered in sand or pebbles (see shore)
beaches (pl)

bridge (n)
something that is built over a river, road or railway so that people can cross
bridges (pl)
(see viaduct and aqueduct)

Geography

city (n)
a large town
cities (pl)

climate (n)
the main type of weather in a region or country

> **Example**
> Britain and Egypt have very different **climates** (pl).

coast (n)
the land next to the sea
coasts (pl)

community (n)
1. a group of people, plants or creatures living in one place
2. a group of people with the same ideas, interests or beliefs
communities (pl)

compass (n)
an instrument with a needle that always points north, used by sailors and others who need to find their way
compasses (pl)

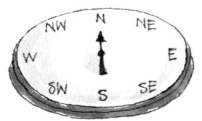

conservation (n)
1. the care of the world's plants, water, landscape and animals
2. the care of objects and buildings from the past

continent (n)
a very large area of land

> **Example**
> The seven **continents** (pl) in the world are:
> 1 Asia, 2 Africa, 3 North America, 4 South America, 5 Antarctica, 6 Europe, 7 Australasia.

country (n)
1. a part of the world with borders around it, usually with its own government
countries (pl)
2. another word for countryside

countryside (n)
areas away from towns and cities, e.g. fields, villages, woods and farms

croft (n)
a small farm in Scotland or the north of England
crofts (pl)

crop (n)
plants such as wheat, fruits or vegetables which are grown for food
crops (pl)

desert (n)
a dry, often sandy area, with few plants

> **Example**
> Camels are used to carry people across **deserts (pl)**.

destination (n)
a place someone or something is travelling to
destinations (pl)

earth (n)
1. the planet we live on
2. the soil that plants grow in

environment (n)
the conditions in which people, plants and animals live
environments (pl)

farm (n)
land and buildings where crops are grown and animals are kept

feature (n)
something special about a place or object

> **Example**
> Waterfalls, streams, river banks and river wildlife are all **features (pl)** of a river.

flood (v)
floods; flooding; flooded
water overflowing onto land

forest (n)
a large area covered in trees
forests (pl)

globe (n)
a round moving object that has a map of the world on it
globes (pl)

hamlet (n)
a small village
hamlets (pl)

hill (n)
a high piece of ground

> **Example**
> The South Downs in Sussex are **hills (pl)**.

holiday (n)
1. time off school or work
2. time spent away from home, for fun
holidays (pl)

home (n)
a place where someone lives
homes (pl)

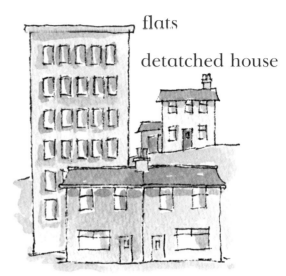

flats

detatched house

semi-detatched house

hotel (n)
a building where people can stay on their holidays
hotels (pl)

house (n)
a building where people live
houses (pl)

human (adj)
something to do with people

> **Example**
> Human geography is the study of the ways people live and work in an area.

industry (n)
the making of goods in factories and working with raw materials such as coal and oil
industries (pl)

inlet (n)
a small bay or opening into a river, sea or lake
inlets (pl)

island (n)
an area of land with water all around it
islands (pl)

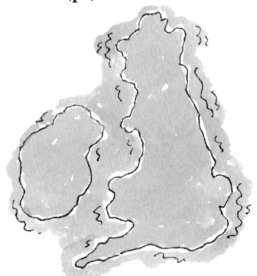

isle (n)
a small island

Example
There are many **isles (pl)** off the coast of Scotland.

lake (n)
a large area of water, usually fresh, with land all around it
lakes (pl)

land (n)
1. the dry part of the Earth
2. another word for country
lands (pl)

landscape (n)
all you can see when you look out over an area of land
landscapes (pl)

leisure (n)
time spent relaxing and having fun

football

dancing

reading

local (adj)
something that is nearby

mainland (n)
the main area of land in a continent
mainlands (pl)

manufacture (v)
manufactures;
manufacturing;
manufactured
to make things on a large scale, using machines

map (n)
a special kind of drawing showing an area's features
maps (pl)

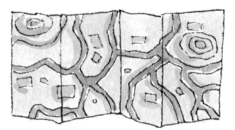

market (n)
a group of stalls where people sell things such as fruit and vegetables, cloths and crafts
markets (pl)

monsoon (n)
strong winds and heavy rainfall in India and South East Asia
monsoons (pl)

mountain (n)
a very high hill
mountains (pl)

occupation (n)
someone's job or work
occupations (pl)

ocean (n)
a very big sea

Example
There are four **oceans** (pl): the Arctic, the Atlantic, the Indian and the Pacific.

office (n)
a building where people work
offices (pl)

park (n)
1. a large green area for walking and playing
2. an area of open countryside with a purpose, such as a wildlife park
parks (pl)

passport (n)
a small book that a person has, that tells other countries who they are and what country they come from
passports (pl)

pedestrian (n)
someone who walks
pedestrians (pl)

physical (adj)
everything to do with the land

plain (n)
a large flat area with few trees and plants
plains (pl)

polar (adj)
to do with the North and South Poles

pollute (v)
pollutes; polluting; polluted
to make things such as the air and water dirty

Pollution (n) is something that pollutes.

pond (n)
a pool of water
ponds (pl)

population (n)
the number of people living in a place

Example
China and India both have large **populations** (pl).

recycle (v)
recycles; recycling; recycled
to turn rubbish into something that can be used again

> **Example**
> Used paper can be recycled and made into toilet paper or kitchen paper.

region (n)
a part of a country or a large area
regions (pl)

river (n)
a wide stream of water that flows into a sea, lake or another river
rivers (pl)

road (n)
a wide track for wheeled vehicles such as cars and lorries
roads (pl)

route (n)
the way you go to get to a place
routes (pl)

rural (adj)
to do with the countryside

scale (n)
the size of things on a map compared to their full size
scales (pl)

sea (n)
a large area of salty water
seas (pl)

seaside (n)
a place or town beside the sea

settlement (n)
a place where people have built a village or town
settlements (pl)

shore (n)
land by the side of a sea or lake
shores (pl)

stream (n)
a small flow of water which goes into a river
streams (pl)

survey (n)
a study of an area or feature such as a river or the local park
surveys (pl)

temperature (n)
how hot or cold an area is

Example
The Arctic and the Sahara Desert have very different **temperatures** (pl).

tide (n)
the movement of the sea towards the land and back
tides (pl)

tourist (n)
someone who is on holiday in another place
tourists (pl)

town (n)
a large settlement, bigger than a village
towns (pl)

trade (v)
trades; trading; traded
buying and selling things

transport (n)
ways of carrying goods and people from place to place, such as railways, cars and aeroplanes

plane

train

ship

car

transport (v)
transports; transporting; transported
to take things or people to another placc

tropical (adj)
a way of describing a very wet and hot climate

urban (adj)
to do with towns or cities

valley (n)
low ground between two hills

> **Example**
> The river flowed through several **valleys (pl)**.

viaduct (n)
a bridge that carries a road or railway over a valley
viaducts (pl)

village (n)
a small settlement found in the countryside
villages (pl)

volcano (n)
a place, usually a mountain, where hot rocks and gas are blown out of the inside of the Earth
volcanoes (pl)

wood (n)
1. a small area covered in trees
woods (pl)
2. the hard material that makes up the trunk and branches of a tree

world (n)
all the Earth and its people
worlds (pl)

Art

architect (n)
someone who plans buildings
architects (pl)

architecture (n) (pl)
the style of a building

art (n)
a painting, drawing or other work created by an artist

The **arts (pl)** also include music, dance and poetry.

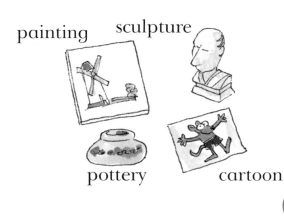

painting   sculpture

pottery   cartoon

art gallery (n)
a place showing works of art
art galleries (pl)

artist (n)
someone who creates art
artists (pl)

assemble (v)
assembles; assembling; assembled
1. to collect parts and tools
2. to put different parts together to make something

background (n)
things in the back of a picture
backgrounds (pl)

> **Example**
> The trees are in the background of the picture.

batik (n)
a craft which uses wax and dye to make a pattern on cloth

blend (v)
blends; blending; blended
to mix things together

> **Example**
> We can blend paint and glue together to make the paint thicker.

block print (n)
a shape or picture on a block of wood or card, used to make prints
block prints (pl)

brush (n)
a tool, usually made from hair or nylon, which is used for painting and decorating things
brushes (pl)

carving (n)
something shaped by a sharp tool
carvings (pl)

chalk (n)
a soft rock made into coloured sticks, used for drawing
chalks (pl)

charcoal (n)
a soft black substance made from burnt wood, used for drawings and rubbings

clay (n)
a wet, thick mud that can be made into different shapes and which goes hard when dried or baked
clays (pl)

collage (n)
a picture made from different materials
collages (pl)

colour wheel (n)
shows a range of colours, how they can be mixed and how they can be used
colour wheels (pl)

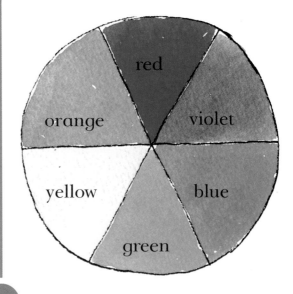

complementary colours (pl)

colours opposite each other on the colour wheel which work well if put next to each other (see colour wheel)

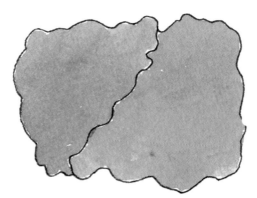

contrast (v)
contrasts; contrasting; contrasted

to show how two or more things are different when put next to each other

craft (n)

something that is made by people, such as by weaving, sewing, woodwork and pottery
crafts (pl)

crayon (n)

a thin, coloured stick made from wax, used for drawings or rubbings
crayons (pl)

create (v)
creates; creating; created

to make something from your own ideas

decorate (v)
decorates; decorating; decorated

1. to paint a room another colour
2. to add colour or other things to an object to make it look nice

design

1. (**n**) a drawing or plan produced before something is made to show how it will look or work
2. (**n**) a pattern or style of something
3. (**v**) **designs; designing; designed**
to draw or plan something

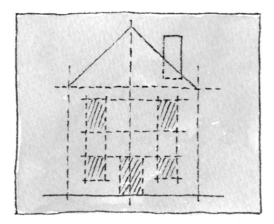

designer (n)
somebody who plans how things are made
designers (pl)

draw (v)
draws; drawing; drew
to make a picture with pens, crayons or pencils

drawing (n)
a picture
drawings (pl)

cartoon drawing

line drawing

cartoon strip drawing

etch (v)
etches; etching; etched
to scratch a design on a surface such as glass, metal or stone with a sharp instrument

fabric (n)
cloth made by people (see weave)
fabrics (pl)

figure (n)
a human or animal shape
figures (pl)

fire (v)
fires; firing; fired
to bake clay in a very hot oven called a kiln

foreground (n)
the front part of a picture
foregrounds (pl)

form (v)
forms; forming; formed
to make something into a shape, object or figure

frame
1. **(n)** something that gives support to a structure
frames (pl)
2. **(v) frames; framing; framed**
to put an edge around a painting or drawing

geometric drawing (n)
a shape or picture made from patterns of lines
geometric drawings (pl)

glaze (n)
a shiny surface on pottery
glazes (pl)

glue (n)
a substance used to stick things together
glues (pl)

kiln (n)
an oven used to bake clay objects to harden them
kilns (pl)

landscape (n)
a picture of the countryside
landscapes (pl)

line (n)
1. the outline or main shape of a picture
2. thin marks
lines (pl)

man-made material (n)
material made by people
man-made materials (pl)

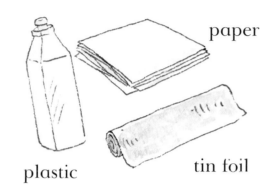

paper

plastic   tin foil

model
1. **(n)** a small copy of something
models (pl)
2. **(v) models; modelling; modelled**
to make something from a material such as clay

mono-print (n)
one print made from a picture
mono-prints (pl)

mosaic (n)
a picture made from small bits of coloured stones or glass
mosaics (pl)

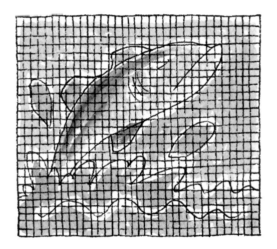

mould (n)
a container which clay can be put into, to form a shape
moulds (pl)

mural (n)
a picture painted onto a wall
murals (pl)

natural material (n)
a material made by nature
natural materials (pl)

observational drawing (n)
a detailed drawing made by looking at something closely
observational drawings (pl)

oil paint (n)
paint mixed with oil to make a thick, rich texture
oil paints (pl)

paint
1. **(n)** coloured liquid for painting pictures, and for decorating
paints (pl)
2. **(v) paints; painting; painted**
to use paints to colour or decorate something

palette (n)
a board on which paint colours are mixed
palettes (pl)

papier-maché (n)
mashed-up paper mixed with glue, which hardens when dry

pastel (n)
1. a soft coloured crayon
2. a picture made from
pastels (pl)
3. a light shade of a colour

pattern (n)
1. a repeated design
2. a design using shapes, colours and lines
3. a model or plan for making something
patterns (pl)

perspective (n)
the way something is drawn to make it look three-dimensional (3-D)
perspectives (pl)

plan (n)
1. a drawing or diagram of something that is to be made
2. how something will be done
plans (pl)

portrait (n)
a drawing or painting of a person
portraits (pl)

pottery (n)
things made from fired clay
pottery (pl)

primary colours (n) (pl)
the main colours from which all other colours come (see colour wheel)

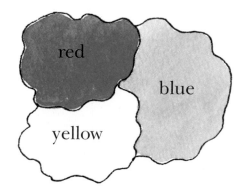

red

blue

yellow

print (v)
prints; printing; printed
to put a design or pattern onto paper or other materials

Art

reclaimed material (n)
material made from left-overs
reclaimed materials (pl)

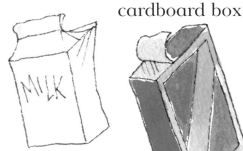

cardboard box

milk carton

margarine tub

rubbing (n)
to put paper over a design or picture and rub over it with soft pencils or crayons to make a copy
rubbings (pl)

scissors (n)
tools for cutting paper or card
scissors (pl)

score (v)
scores, scoring, scored
to mark lines using a sharp tool to fold card or thin wood

sculptor (n)
someone who carves three-dimensional statues and shapes out of materials such as stone
sculptors (pl)

sculpture (n)
three-dimensional shapes and statues made out of stone, wood or other materials
sculptures (pl)

secondary colour (n)
a colour that can be made by mixing two primary colours together
secondary colours (pl)

self-portrait (n)
a drawing or painting of an artist done by him or her self
self-portraits (pl)

sew (v)
sews; sewing; sewed
to mend, make or decorate cloth using a needle and thread

shade (v)
shades; shading; shaded
to darken drawings or pictures using pencils, pens or paint

sketch
1. **(n)** a rough outline or idea for a design or picture
sketches (pl)
2. **(v) sketches; sketching; sketched**
to draw a rough sketch

stencil (n)
a thin material with a pattern of holes cut in it; painting over these holes forms a pattern on the surface underneath

> **Example**
> The artist created a book of shapes and patterns made from **stencils (pl)**.

still-life (n)
a drawing or painting of objects that don't move, such as flowers or fruit
still-lifes (pl)

template (n)
a shape that can be drawn or cut around
templates (pl)

> **Example**
> Charlie is drawing around a star template to make a decoration.

textile (n)
fabric that has been woven
(see weaving)
textiles (pl)

texture (n)
what we feel when we touch
something, such as a fabric
or other material

> **Example**
> The rugs all had different
> **textures (pl)**.

thread (n)
a thin string of material such
as cotton, used for sewing
threads (pl)

three-dimensional (adj)
something that has length,
breadth and depth

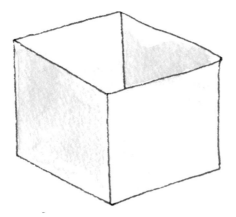

tint (n)
a very pale colour, or one
that has white added to it
tints (pl)

tone (n)
how light or dark a colour is
tones (pl)

trace (v)
traces; tracing; traced
to follow or go over an
outline of a picture or design

two-dimensional (adj)
something that has length
and breadth but no depth

watercolour (n)
1. paints mixed with water
2. a painting using **water
colours (pl)**

weave (v)
weaves; weaving; wove
to make fabric by crossing
different yarns on a loom

Music

audience (n)
a group of people who watch
or listen to a performance
audiences (pl)

beat (n)
the rhythm of a piece of music
beats (pl)

brass instrument (n)
a musical instrument made
using a metal pipe, which the
player blows down to make
musical notes
brass instruments (pl)

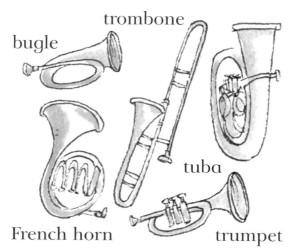

bugle
trombone
tuba
French horn
trumpet

choir (n)
a large group of singers
choirs (pl)

clap (v)
claps; clapping; clapped
to make a sound or a rhythm
by bringing both hands
together

composer (n)
someone who writes music
composers (pl)

concert (n)
a musical performance
concerts (pl)

conductor (n)
someone who makes sure an
orchestra or a choir follows
the music correctly
conductors (pl)

drum (n)
a musical instrument that is
beaten to make a rhythm

Example
The many **drums (pl)**
made a loud noise.

Music

duet (n)
music played or sung by
two people
duets (pl)

guitar (n)
an instrument with six strings
guitars (pl)

harmony (n)
different musical notes that
go well together when played
or sung at the same time
harmonies (pl)

hum (v)
hums; humming; hummed
to make a sound in the
throat with both lips closed

hymn (n)
a religious song
hymns (pl)

instrument (n)
something you play to make
a musical sound
instruments (pl)

key (n)
1. something you press on an
instrument, e.g. a piano, to
make a sound
2. musical sounds based
around one musical note
keys (pl)

keyboard instrument (n)
a musical instrument played by
pressing keys

Example
Organs are **keyboard
instruments (pl)**.

organ   accordion

piano

electronic keyboard

lyrics (n) (pl)
the words in a song

melody (n)
the part of a tune that has
a harmony
melodies (pl)

metre (n)
the main rhythm in music
metres (pl)

musician (n)
someone who plays music
musicians (pl)

notation (n)
a system of symbols for
musical notes
notations (pl)

note (n)
a musical sound
notes (pl)

orchestra (n)
musicians playing different
instruments together
orchestras (pl)

**percussion
instrument (n)**
an instrument you hit or shake
percussion instruments (pl)

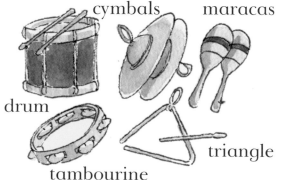

cymbals   maracas

drum

triangle

tambourine

perform (v)
**performs; performing;
performed**
to act, sing or play music to
an audience

performance (n)
a show for an audience

> **Example**
> There were several very
> good **performances (pl)**.

pitch (n)
how high or low a sound is
pitches (pl)

recorder (n)
a kind of musical instrument
like a wooden pipe, that a
player blows through
recorders (pl)

rehearse (v)
**rehearses; rehearsing;
rehearsed**
to practise for a performance

rhythm (n)
the regular beat in a piece of music or a poem
rhythms (pl)

scale (n)
a full set of eight notes
scales (pl)

sing (v)
sings; singing; sung/sang
to make music with your voice

solo (n)
music played or sung by one person
solos (pl)

song (n)
music with words that can be sung
songs (pl)

stave (n)
the five lines on which notes are written (see notes)
staves (pl)

stringed instrument (n)
a musical instrument played by touching its strings
stringed instruments (pl)

sitar

cello   violin   harp

tempo (n)
the speed of a piece of music
tempos (pl)

tune (n)
a simple piece of music
tunes (pl)

volume (n)
how loud or soft a sound is
volumes (pl)

wind instrument (n)
a musical instrument that you blow through
wind instruments (pl)

xylophone (n)
a musical instrument made of wooden blocks, each of which makes a note when hit
xylophones (pl)

application (n)
a computer program that lets you do things such as writing
applications (pl)

attachment (n)
a file that is added to an email (see file and clip art)
attachments (pl)

CD-ROM (n)
a compact disc used in a computer
CD-ROMs (pl)

clip art (n)
ready-drawn pictures and symbols that are found in computer software
clip art (pl)

clipboard (n)
a store of pictures or information made so these can be moved to another file
clipboards (pl)

compact disc (n)
a small circle of plastic that can store information
compact discs (pl)

cursor (n)
a symbol that can be moved around the screen using the mouse
cursors (pl)

data (n) (pl)
the information on documents

database (n)
all the information stored in the computer
databases (pl)

delete (v)
deletes; deleting; deleted
to remove unwanted words and files from a computer

digital (adj)
something which works by giving out and getting electronic signals

digital radio

digital camera

document (n)
work done on the computer such as writing, drawing, graphs and tables
documents (pl)

download (v)
downloads; downloading; downloaded
to move Internet information onto the computer

edit (v)
edits; editing; edited
to correct or change words or sentences

email
1. **(n)** the system of sending or receiving messages or files between computers
2. **(n)** messages sent by email
emails (pl)
3. **(v) emails; emailing; emailed**
to send or receive messages from one computer to another

fax (n)
a document which is copied and sent electronically
faxes (pl)

file (n)
information stored under a given name
files (pl)

folder (n)
where different computer files are stored
folders (pl)

font (n)
a design for the letters, symbols and numbers used in a document

> **Example**
> You can use many different **fonts (pl)** in one magazine.

You can have text in:

different styles

You can have text in:

italic and underlined

Times

You can set the text or symbols in different sizes:

small   medium   large

hardware (n) (pl)
things that you can touch such as the computer and the keyboard

icon (n)
a picture or symbol used to show a file or application
icons (pl)

Internet (n)
the system that lets computers around the world connect up to each other and share information

key (n)
a button on a computer keyboard
keys (pl)

keyboard (n)
the set of keys used with the computer
keyboards (pl)

menu (n)
a list of programs, applications and files
menus (pl)

IT

mouse (n)
a hand-held object which is used to move the cursor

network (n)
a set of computers connected together
networks (pl)

paste (v)
pastes; pasting; pasted
to move text or pictures from one place to another

program (n)
the instructions that tell the computer what to do
programs (pl)

return (n)
the key that sends the cursor to the next line of a document

save (v)
saves; saving; saved
to store data made in a document

software (n)
programs that can be used on a computer
software (pl)

space bar (n)
the long key on the keyboard that makes spaces between words
space bars (pl)

space bar

surf (v)
surfs; surfing; surfed
to look at different websites on the Internet

toolbar (n)
a row of buttons on the computer screen
toolbars (pl)

website (n)
pages of information on the Internet that can be reached and read using a computer

> **Example**
> Ladybird's website is full of fun and games. You can find it at www.ladybird.com

Time

morning
midday
noon
afternoon
dusk
evening
night
midnight
yesterday
today
tomorrow

Days

Monday
Tuesday
Wednesday
Thursday
Friday
Saturday
Sunday

Months

January
February
March
April
May
June
July
August
September
October
November
December

Seasons

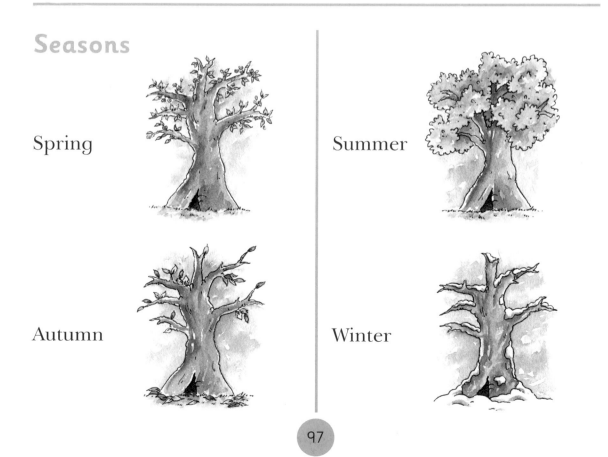

Spring

Summer

Autumn

Winter

Numbers

Cardinal numbers

0 nought/zero
1 one
2 two
3 three
4 four
5 five
6 six
7 seven
8 eight
9 nine
10 ten
11 eleven
12 twelve
13 thirteen
14 fourteen
15 fifteen
16 sixteen
17 seventeen
18 eighteen
19 nineteen
20 twenty
21 twenty-one
30 thirty
31 thirty-one
40 forty
41 forty-one
50 fifty
51 fifty-one
60 sixty
61 sixty-one
70 seventy
71 seventy-one
80 eighty
81 eighty-one
90 ninety
91 ninety-one
100 one hundred
200 two hundred
1000 one thousand
1,000,000 one million

Ordinal numbers

1st first
2nd second
3rd third
4th fourth
5th fifth
6th sixth
7th seventh
8th eighth
9th ninth
10th tenth
11th eleventh
12th twelfth
20th twentieth
100th hundredth
1000th thousandth

Length

mm millimetres
$10mm = 1cm$
cm centimetres
$100cm = 1m$
m metres
$1000m = 1km$
km kilometres

Weight

mg milligrams
$1000mg = 1g$
g grams
$1000g = 1kg$
kg kilograms

Capacity

ml millilitres
$10ml = 1cl$
cl centilitres
$100cl = 1l$
l litres

Words

Question words

How
What
When
Where
Who
Why
Which

Nouns

the name of something, e.g.
tree
house
car
school

Proper nouns

names of people or places
beginning with a capital
letter, e.g.
Andrew
Lauren
London
Paris

Adjectives

describe a thing, e.g.
beautiful
nasty
lucky
difficult

Adverbs

describe an action, e.g.
quickly
well
strongly
nicely

Prefixes

anti-	opposite or against
co-	together with something else
de-	to take something away
dis-	opposite
ex-	in the past
in/im-	opposite
micro-	very small
mid-	in the middle
mini-	very small
mis-	badly or wrongly
non-	opposite
pre-	before
re-	again
semi-	half
sub-	under
super-	more/bigger
un-	opposite

Shapes

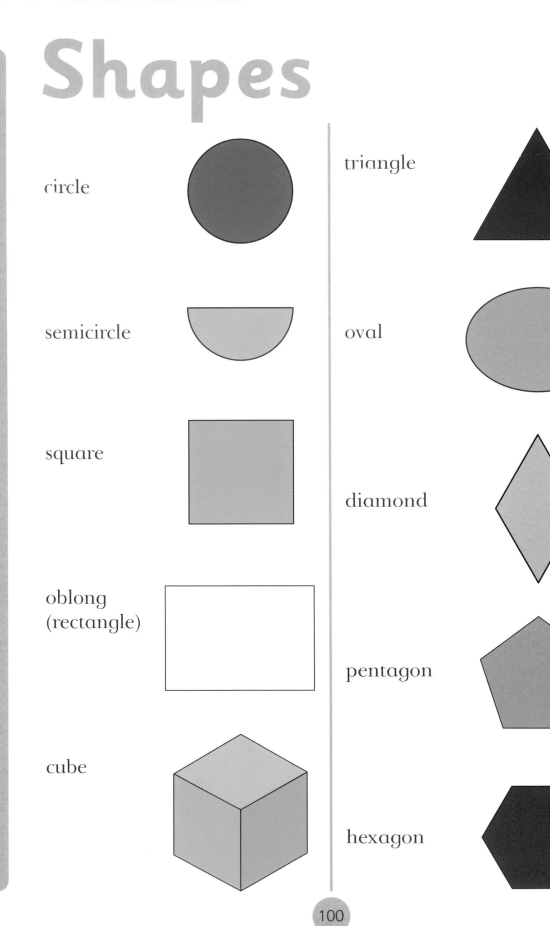

circle

semicircle

square

oblong
(rectangle)

cube

triangle

oval

diamond

pentagon

hexagon

Colours

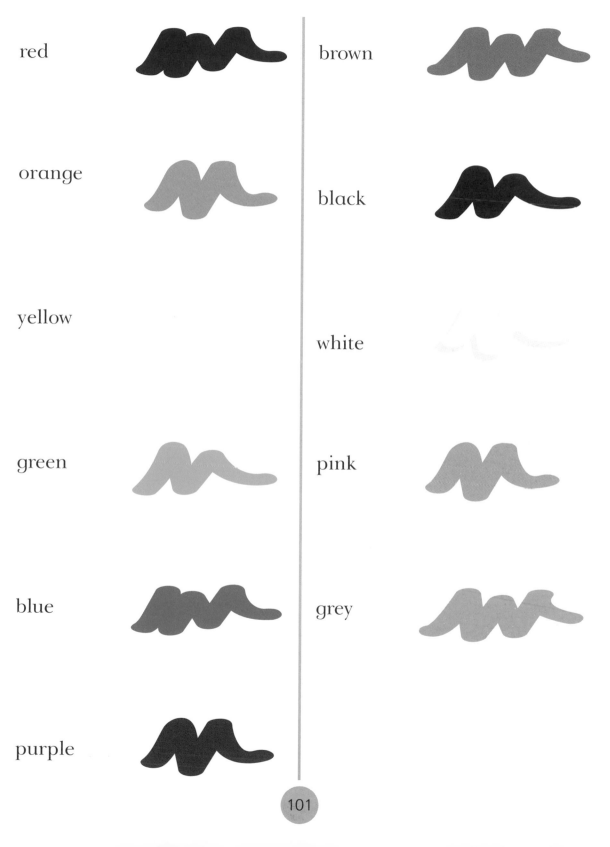

red

orange

yellow

green

blue

purple

brown

black

white

pink

grey

Antonyms

Antonyms are words that mean the opposite.

above   below

awake   asleep

begin   end

before   after

top   bottom

open   closed

2
4
6
8
10

even

1
3
5
7
9

odd

deep

shallow

fast

slow

up

down

over

under

happy

sad